MAZE

Vol 11

Ages 4-6

FOR KIDS

MAZE BOOK

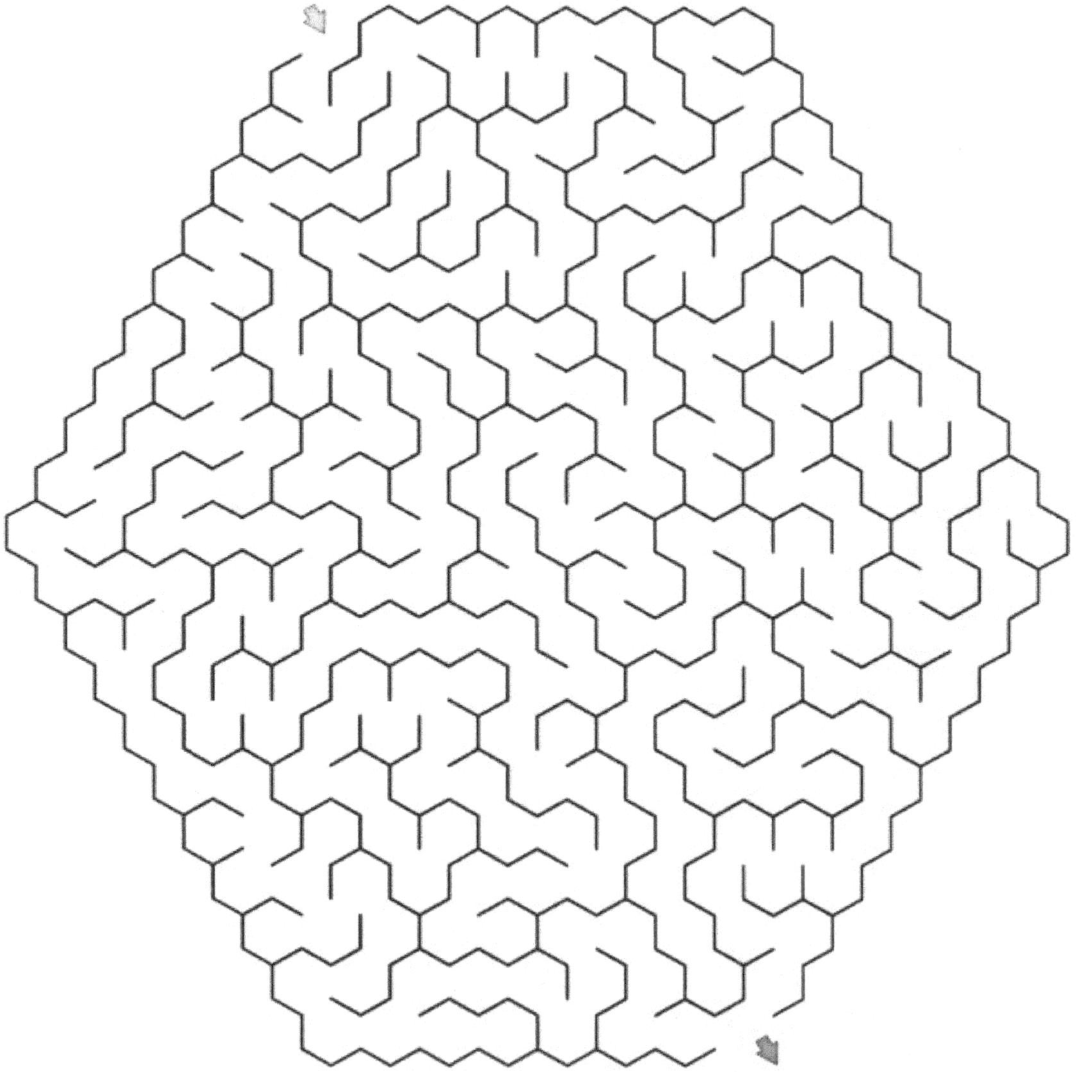

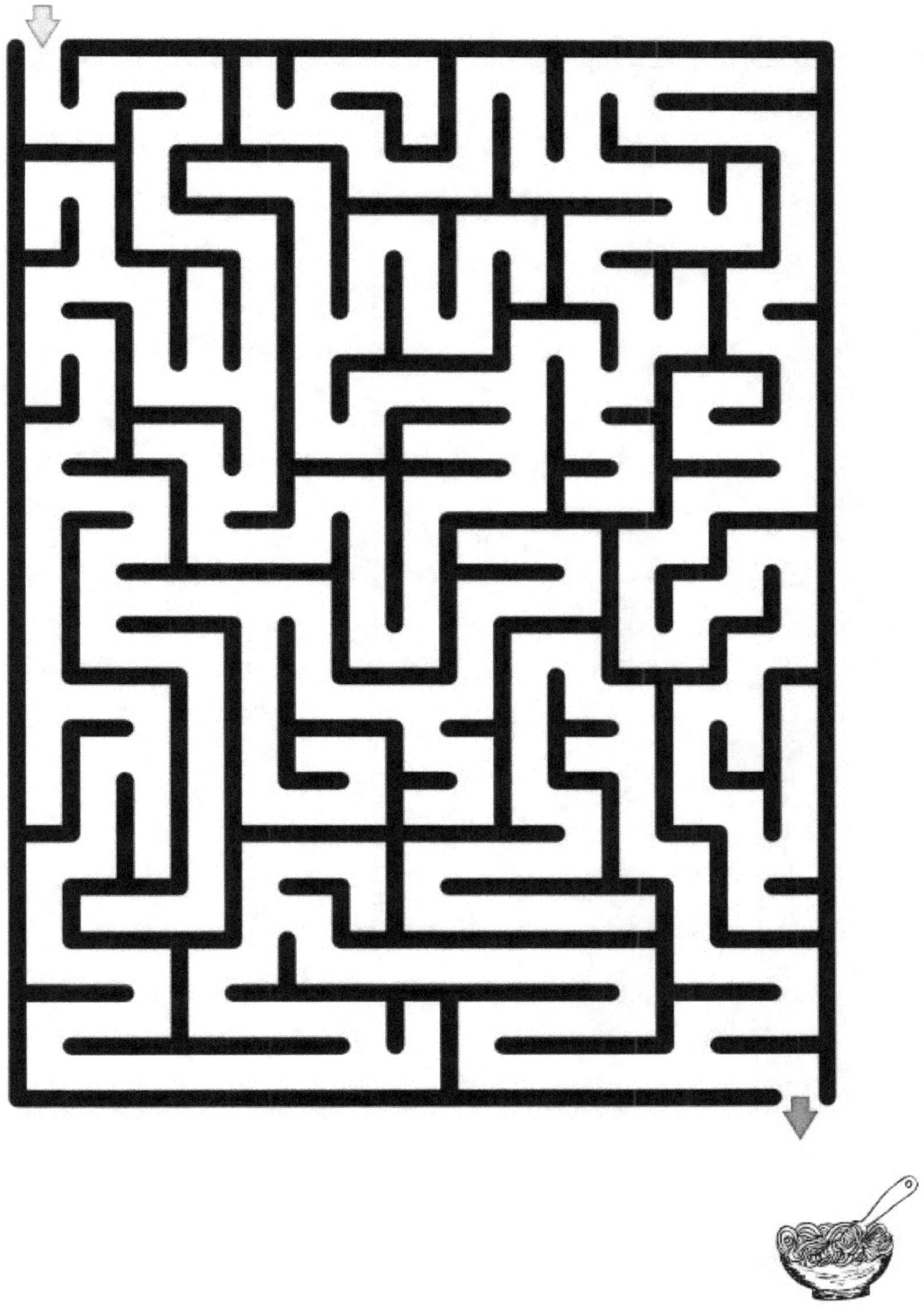

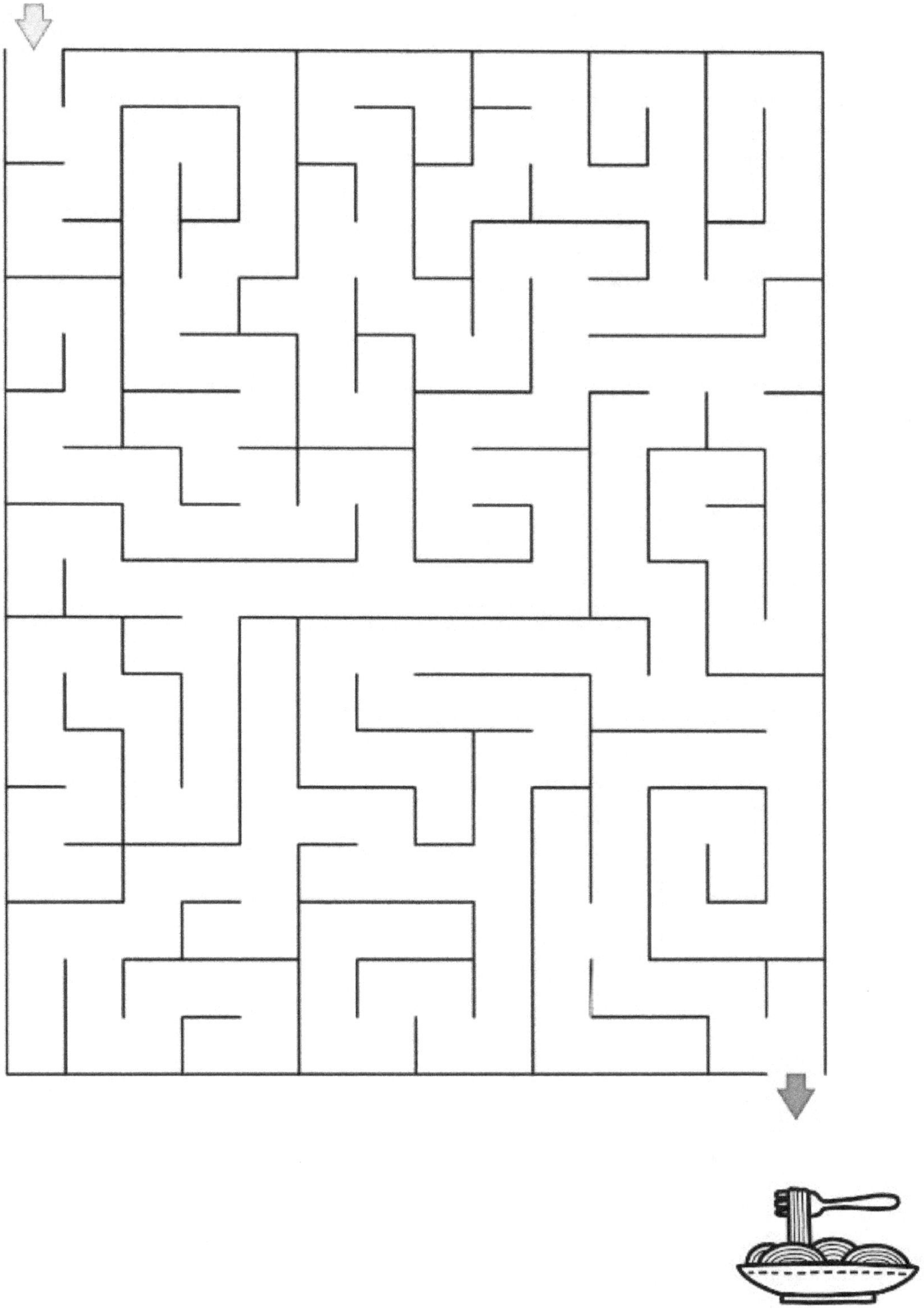

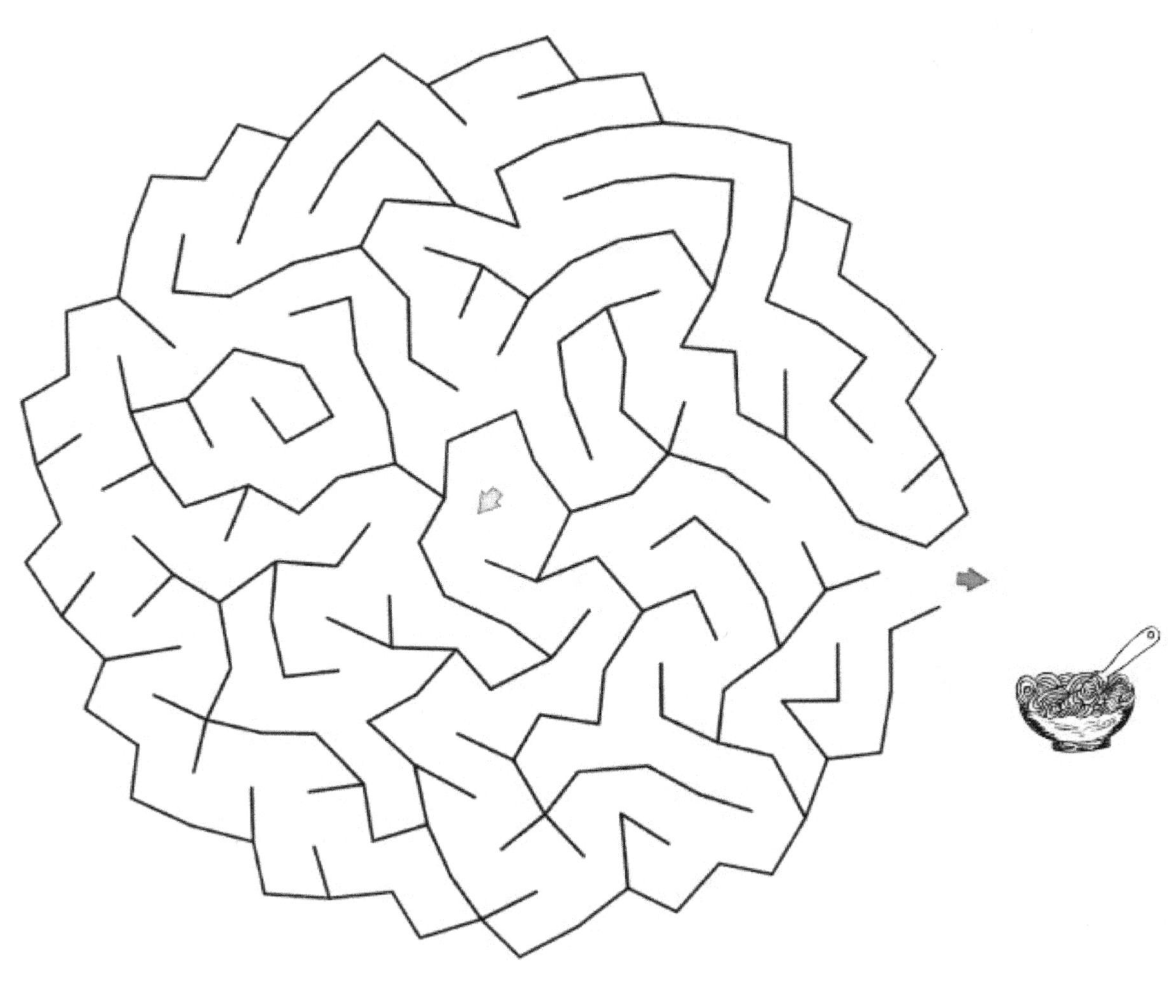

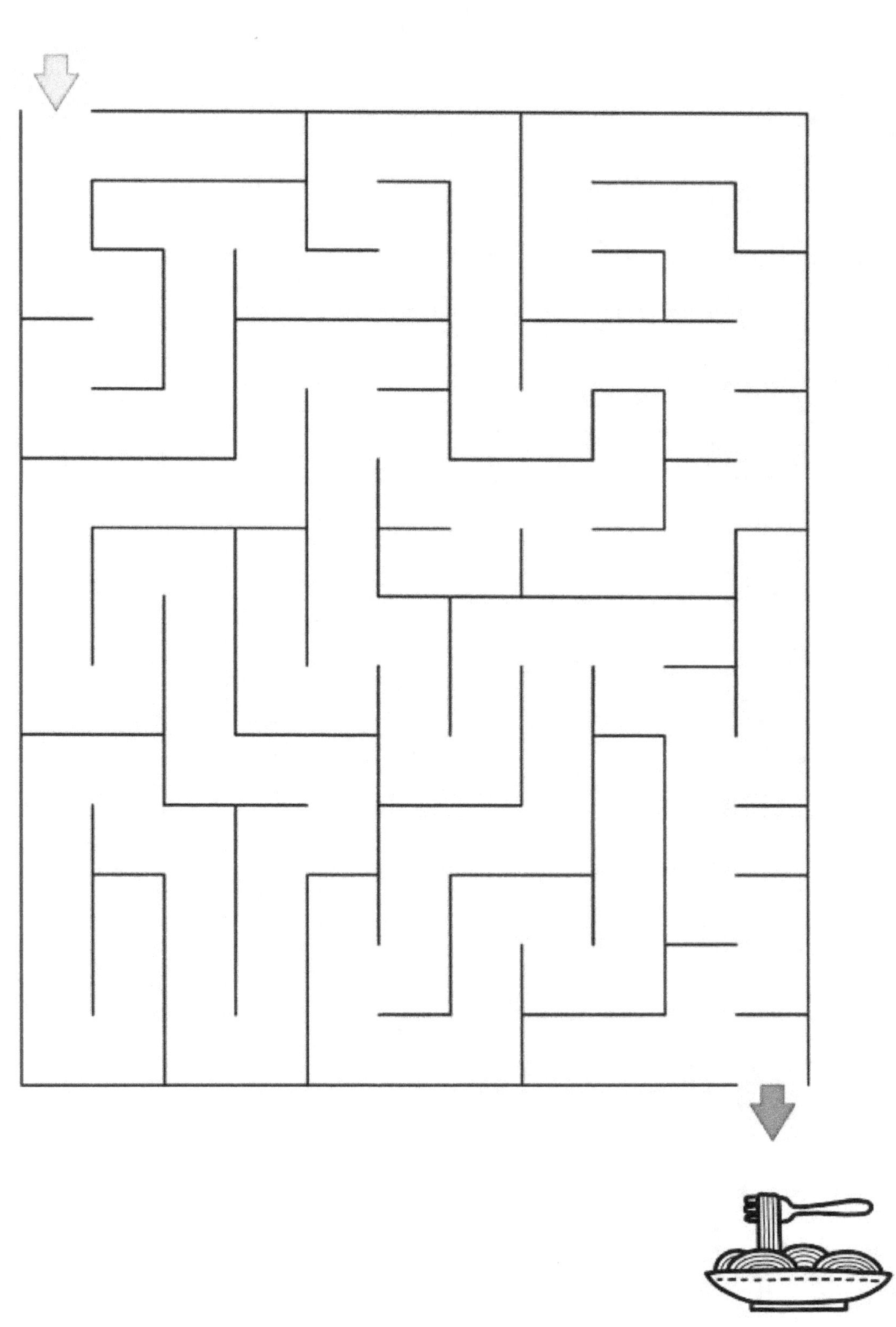

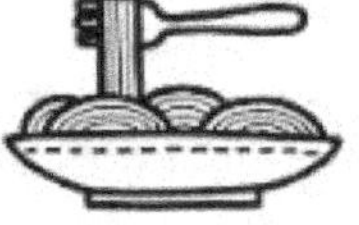

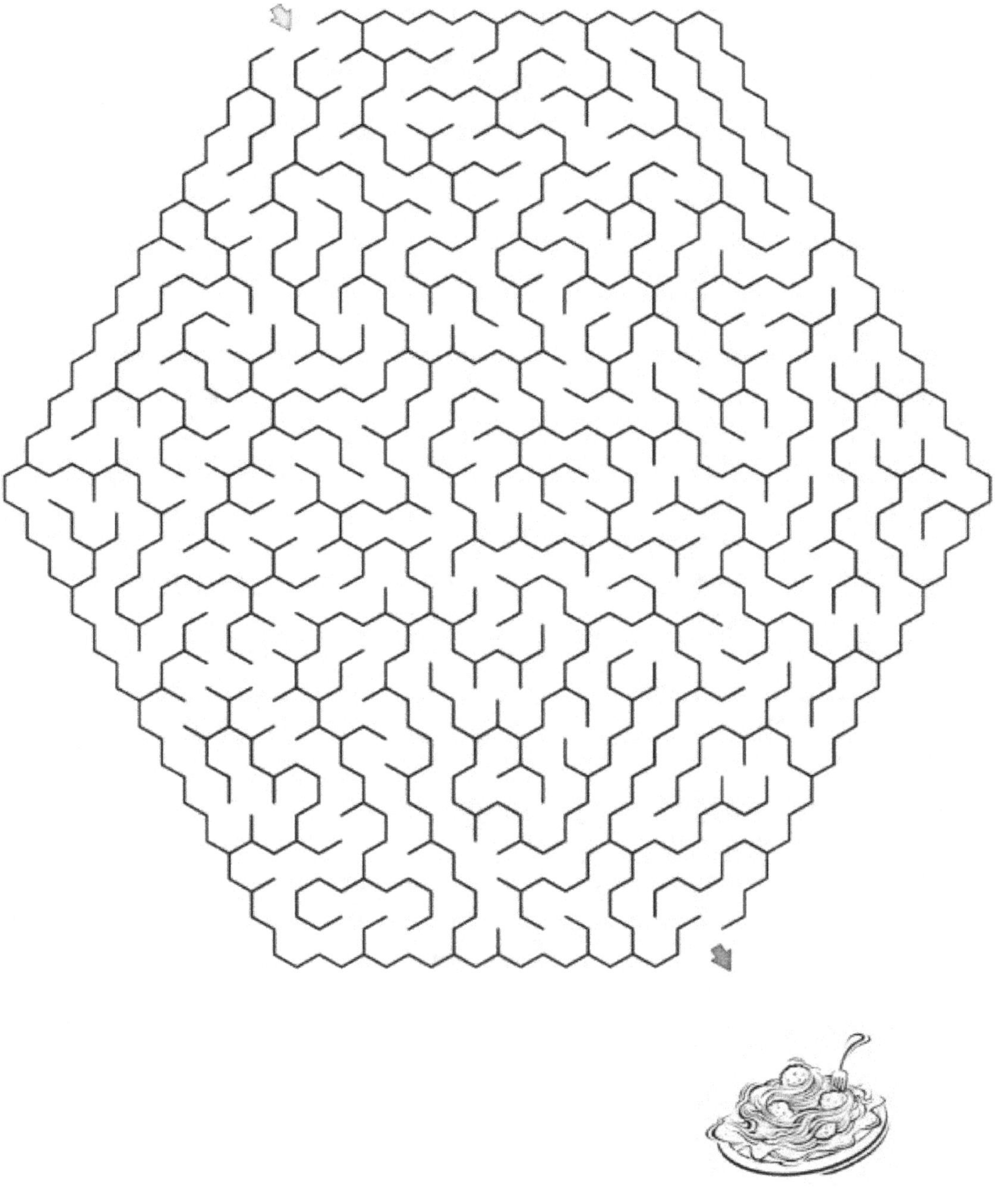

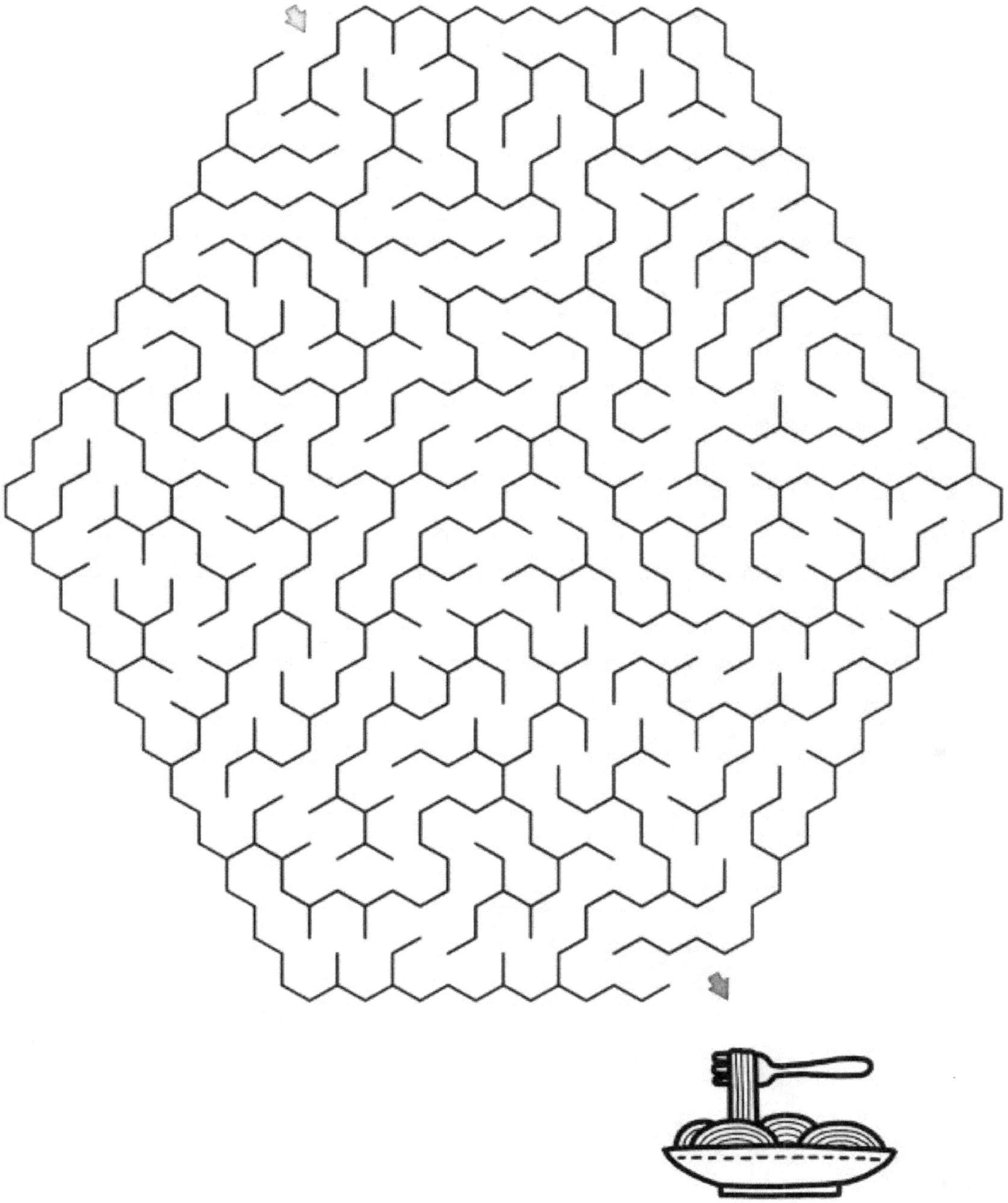

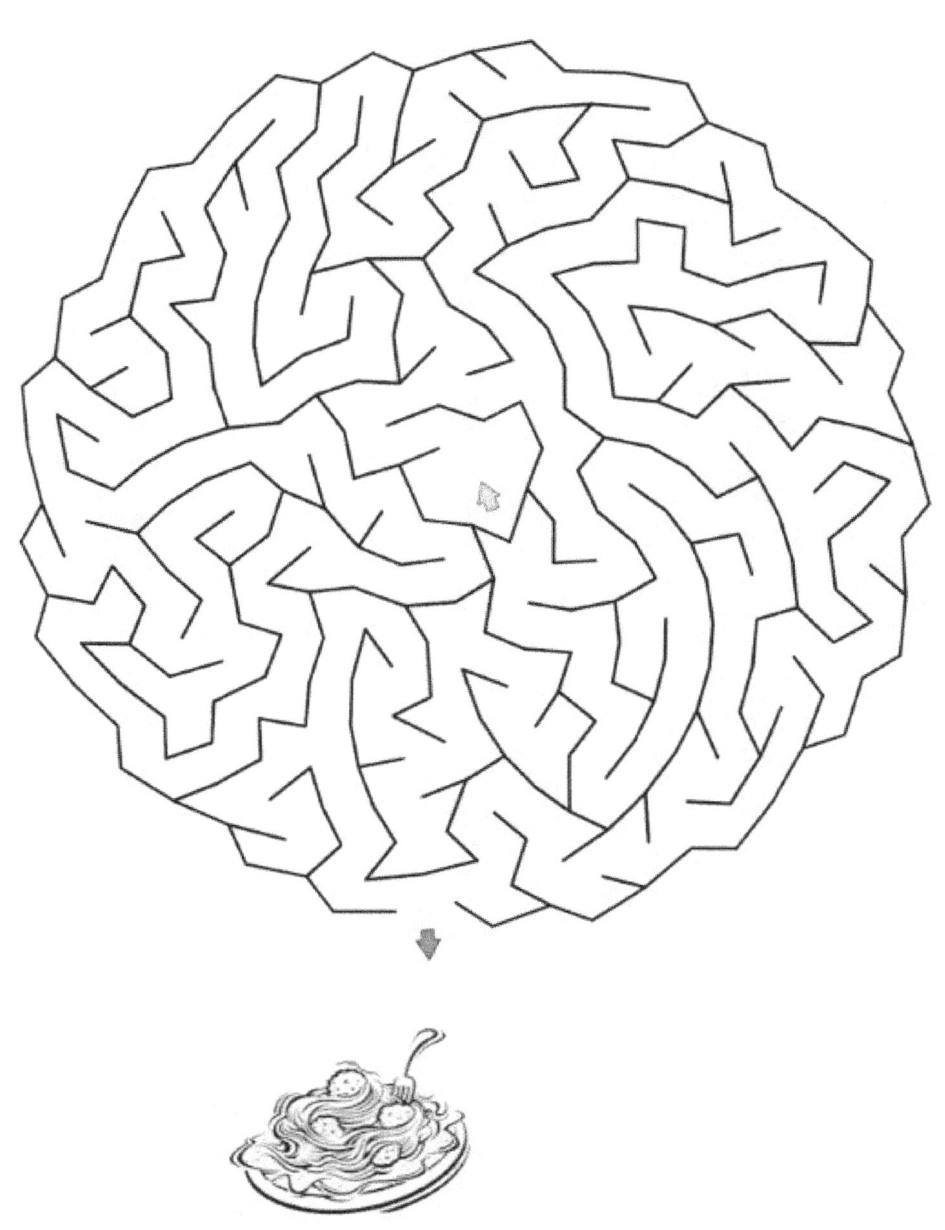

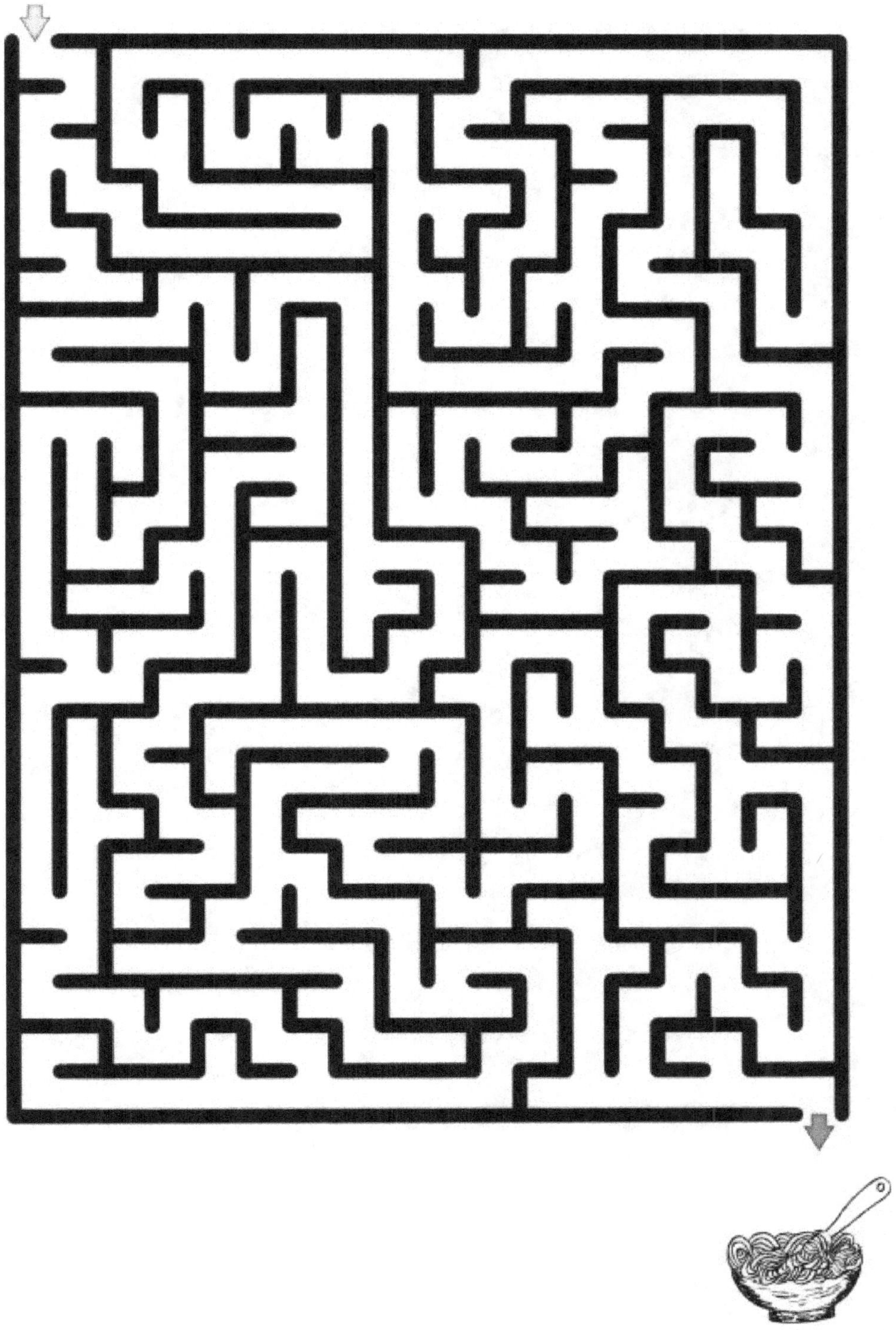

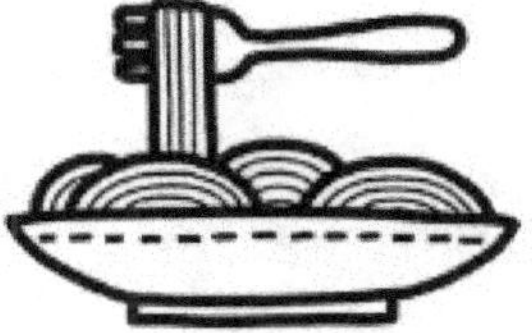

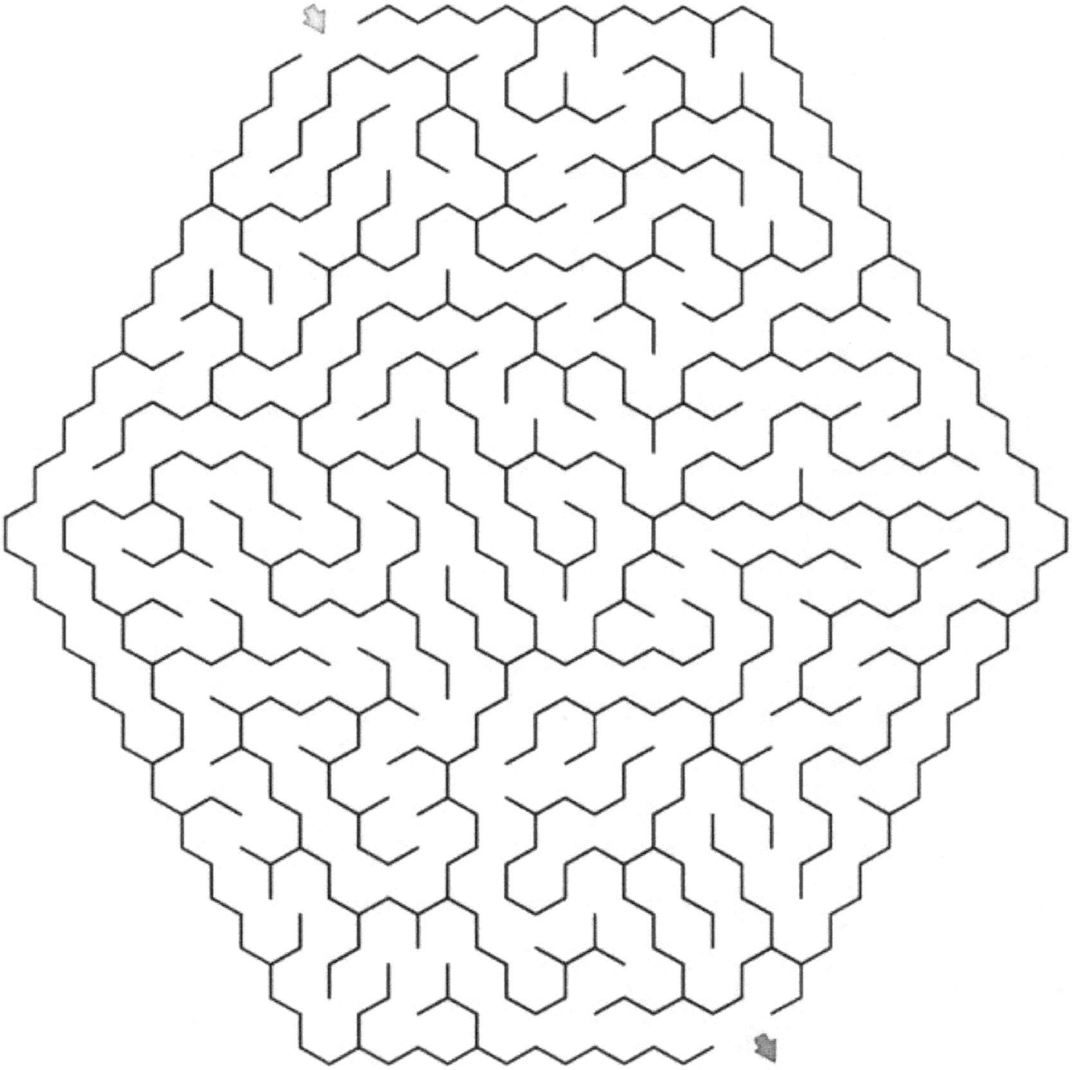

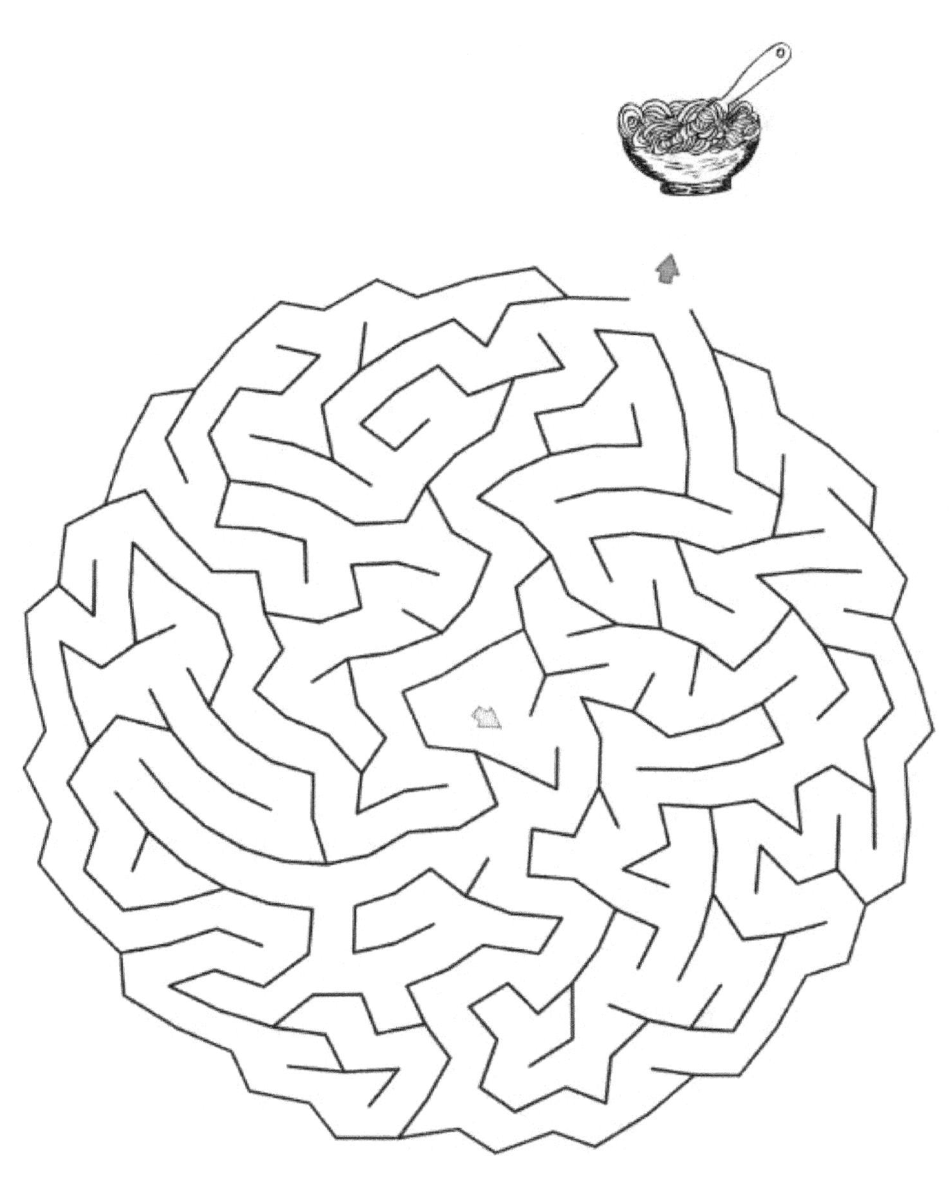